This is your real name

This is your real name

Elizabeth Morton

OTAGO UNIVERSITY PRESS
Te Whare Tā o Te Wānanga o Ōtākou

Some of these poems have been previously published in *Atlanta Review*, *Narrative Magazine*, *Poetry New Zealand Yearbook 2017*, *Bonsai: Best small stories from Aotearoa New Zealand*, *New Welsh Review*, *Literary Orphans*, *Apeiron Review*, *Cleaver Magazine*, *Crannog Magazine*, *Black Fox Literary Magazine*, *The American Journal of Poetry*, the NZPS anthology *The Unnecessary Invention of Punctuation* and *Intima: A Journal of Narrative Medicine*. In the poem 'How I hate Pokémon but I can show restraint and just talk about my adolescence', one line has been taken from the internet and repurposed.

Published by Otago University Press
Te Whare Tā o Te Wānanga o Ōtakou
Level 1, 398 Cumberland Street
Dunedin, New Zealand
university.press@otago.ac.nz
www.otago.ac.nz/press

First published 2019
Copyright © Elizabeth Morton
The moral rights of the author have been asserted.

ISBN 978-1-98-853192-2

Editor: Anna Hodge
Design and layout: Fiona Moffat
Author photograph: Natalie Morgan

Cover: Iqi Qoror, *Child Play. The Swing*, 2016, acrylic, charcoal and wool on canvas, 150 x 110cm.

Printed by Southern Colour Print, Dunedin.

*For people who wait
and people who
are alone.*

Contents

Untouch

They said *write it anonymously*. This is my real name.
They said don't you dare pigeonhole. I am a tendril of a boy.
My handshake is a riddle, my memory of gardens
turns in on itself like a wentletrap shell. I remember honeysuckle
like it was a Tuesday in November. My mother
crushed sweet flowers on my pillowslip. It was yolk sun
and leached through my cloth, down to my calamari meat.
They said keep the cat in the bag. They said swallow your name
hook, line and sinker. Hold your three hearts in your horror mouth.
I was garbage, in another life; I was a tarpaulin, holding everything in.
I was the muscular sack, inked words pulsing through the deep.
I was hydrosphere and trembling in the heat. *Kraken Kraken.*
I remember my life in gardens that rise above the seawall.
This is my real name. The thing I cannot touch.

After

Sometimes, it is enough to close your eyes.
All those campfires, sitting by with guitars and ouija boards and Xanax.
All that freedom we yodelled that ricocheted back, through the gaps in
    the tea-trees.
Teeth that dark lisps through, gardens that hold grief in their hedging.
Night comes apart, like everything else.
We know the landmarks for their hardness.
There were times I would walk the weed-bank, looking for you
in shadows, in the starflowers that light the dirt road home.
When I told you about the last polar bear in Auckland Zoo
it was the final thing you'd think about this world—
the image of one yellowed bear pacing his cell, while the credits go down,
but I wouldn't know that until later. Later was too late
to tell you how a woman sewed a wing back on a butterfly
and how I saw it fly on the video, and thought of the way
you are always hovering above people,
beside people, away from people, but always up.
Sometimes, it hurts to open your eyes. These things happened:
The polar bear did a figure-of-eight on the warm concrete.
The butterfly caught on the windscreen of a haulage truck.
Ice caps melted in my hands and the waters rose by inches
when I dumped my sorrow in the Atlantic. Somebody said
Maybe it's not happening and there was a standing ovation
as our outdoor furniture floated down the street.
There are some truths we don't need to steer by.
When I open my eyes I'm in the same cage I was in yesterday.
I am the same yellow bear driving the same haulage truck
over ice sheets, thin as a prince's hairline.
What night is this? We talk about the butterfly like it got away.
We talk about you, like you are here. Like you never left.

Inside-out

Here, there is no wood stack, no lorry trucks that grind the gravel.

There is no spitting into the wind, no weathervane bird to summon storms.

There are no sheep that mew about ancestral stone. There is no stone.

There is no running through the asparagus stalks and gorse and clover.

She cannot run. The front door is bolted shut. Skylines taunt her from their haunches.

Her head is in the sand, but neither dune bugs or silt hoppers meet her there.

People move like cattle, somnolent and black eyed, along the linoleum.

There is no marauding buzzard. The moon is all solipsism and nothing else.

People look through the shatterproof glass, and think they see a man there.

Is there a man there? Here, there is no answer but the monotony of sirens,

dull to the gum ear and the gum eye. The woman with the lanyard and key

is not your mother, is not a mammal, but sharpens her beak with a maternal shudder.

There is no touching the black heat at the centre of things.

Outside and inside—a wreckage of stars.

On hold

I can hold
my breath
for three minutes flat
in the superstore aisle
between woks
and waffle irons
screaming catchphrases
in my head or
buying pillows
at the counter
like it's underwater
wrong chemicals
curdling
in my lungs and
the jukebox
playing songs
that make me drowsy
like Radiohead
on ukulele
over the
loudspeaker
the manager keeps
banging on
about
battery eggs
on special
and I'm like
can't you see
bitch
I'm trying to
kill myself
in aisle five

but I'm too
dizzy
even to grab
a lemon squeezer
from the middle shelf

Gap

You might make it, if you sprint.

We run with our hands in pockets.
We are pink dots on an aerial photograph
gapping it through the seafields. I am running
out of ideas. All the honeybees are dead and here we are
packing cargo into thought bubbles. It's like it never
happened. The oceans did not rise up and claim us.
The hooks we cast didn't return broken bottles with SOSs.
We were not rehearsing defeat with every gesture.

We run with our suitcases, dredging a maze
of pesticides and flotsam. We beat through
waterlogged scarecrows, zigzag the salted orange trees,
whistle at muttonbirds as we whizz by. The world
is a smudged thumbprint. Saline. Everything is moving
away from us. By the time we reach the starting block
it's ten past midnight. When the pistol fires,
nobody knows in which direction to run.

You can't, always

I'm not going to cry. All winter the television
sulks in the corner of our love. You put the lentils
in a colander to flush the ugly bits. You peel oranges
to their pith and talk about your past like it was mine too.
You say it was sunnier in Cheltenham than it could ever be
in an unhappy kitchen with a lover made of feathers.
I want to tell you about the way a man can look down
a corridor, the way a hunter visits his scope. There are things
too big to fold into your hands. A barbule is enough
to demonstrate how even soft things fall down,
like small people from towers that trade in shadows.
When I say *I need you*, it clambers up a stairwell in my throat
like you were the only window left in 110 levels of pain.
I'm not going to say I get it. You toss the lentils
in a brine pot and power up the television.
You say we spend too much of life watching
the kind of comedies that make you sad. Like *Home Improvement*
and *The Cosby Show* that make you think of time
and the way we were happy in Cheltenham
before small people sat on window ledges, before
the hunter's scope settled on an ordinary bird.
I'm not going to cry. All morning chopping onions,
watching Bill Cosby hug his wife in Brooklyn Heights
before he was a rapist, and before you first registered
towers on the skyline by their absence.
When I say *I need you* I am a soft thing falling
on something familiar, and it is violence
in the way dispassionate surgery is violence
or the way *The Cosby Show* is what you get
before you get what you never wanted.
   I'll take what I can.

Aubade with hold music

The phone booth was skull-cracked,
        and caulked with soggy directories.
All the people
   we'd never know.
We stood about, like white teeth,
       watching the morning split hairs
in the shattered glass.
       Every other boy was listening to hold music,
every other boy was slipping dollars into the coin slot,
       buying time with small change.

I know you want your mother's dial tone
   like you want a KFC box
or an afternoon of cartoon animals.
   The morning smelled like fire,
like the sun projecting simple stories
   against the warehouse brickwork
and I wonder whether you know
   you are melting.
Writing a poem is a political act.
   I want you to know, what you feel
is more than politics.

The morning sets you apart
like a sapling in the blackwood forest.
   This poem sets you apart, and
you are a small forest pressed against a city.
   You are a small boy,
pulling a measuring tape around a hole
   so big, you can't see the other side.
The morning is a mumbled promise.
   We try the White Pages
for a vein we might tap.

   You pray, into the receiver,
with your eyes open.

The chair

Yellow Mama is buying furniture from Ikea,
rummaging through side tables and ergonomic seats.
She is looking for something with corners.
Yellow Mama loves Alabama children.
She makes the best slaw in Montgomery.
She wears tennis shoes in the sorghum fields.
Yellow Mama has family values.
Yellow Mama has an electrode on her left leg.
Yellow Mama is a choice between negatives,
a cradle between the rock and the hard place.
Yellow Mama jolts her babies to sleep.
Boy, Yellow Mama smokes like a chimney,
and naps in an attic in her sundress—
her children tippytoe past.
Yellow Mama is yellow as a cob of
Alabama corn, or the yolk of a quail egg.
but they can't see that.
She is looking for something with corners.
Her children go up in flames.

Hay, we're on fire!

Girl, we sat in the dog smoke, huffing night and star winks, from
    God's raw hands.
We burned the bales dropped by trucks headed south—
sniffed black yeast and honey straw whiskers.
Girl, we made shadow puppets in the glare—double finger geese,
    and honking circles.
Fire engines spent themselves like serpents on the singed lawn.
Accelerant bled into the grass webs and flooded the gaps between
    the hillock's little toes.
Girl, we charted ridgelines, yabbered stories gone-to-seed to the
    earth's crude fontanels.
Girl, can you feel hallowed fonts that smoulder in our speech
    bubbles?
    I am an Italics kid.
I know how to bat my eyelashes into the prevailing wind.
I can count in sevens with my lids shut.
I know how to meet toothache with a pistol, how to fan fire with
    my small hope.
Girl, on this earth, you can place a knuckle between one skull plate
    and the next.
You can pause in a field of blazing lupin and wonder at the heat.
You know, with you I was dog smoke breathed backwards.
I was the name of the flower you forgot to pick,
but I could prove your lungfuls in algebra, and I could toast your
    birthday
with bourbon in a slandered cup.
Girl, there is violence in these meadows, and blisters on God's raw
    hands.
I could tell you the name of the song you didn't want,
and the vintage of scorched soil that hugs our unborn children.
I could lay a jump sheet outside your shattered window, quench
    your gardens with milk,

let you feed on a nozzle of orange.

Girl, I could be black flame in a yellowed Polaroid.

I could be the shadow geese, the scent of burned feathers, the fumbling
apparition to lead you home.

lucid

i wake among the Times New Roman of my therapist's credentials,
and crawl outside on tines of bone, lifting red meat like hands.
i carry my antlers in a knapsack, with a horsewhip and a coronal map.

                there are warning signs
i should know by now—

the polystyrene beans that spill from my mouth instead of nouns.
the sawdust that scabs my lips.
metaphors that metastasise into flowers, that in turn become
white lies, white lilies.
               i wake in a poem
of my own making.

i have a knife, a head full of splinters,
hip-deep in the bog bed shucked out to settle these words in.

               i'm dreaming now but i wake
too old to know better.

i'm a copycat of ghosts who wait up by curtain tracks,
tapping at their watches,
ghosts who hang like piñatas,
who summon violence to suspend the monotony of living rooms and
    stairs.
i can plagiarise the death throes of a lampshade whose bulk is igneous,
whose eyeball is remorseless like the moon.

              we are all dead here.
i shift a barstool in my sleep.
i flick the hall light switch
while my teeth fall

into my mother's cupped hands.

               hang in there, she says,

and i do i do—i always land on my feet.

i have one or two regrets &

      i want to speak the shame of a crayon at midnight,
of sky that ripens without willing,
      the soft terrorism of city lights that fracture
against the windshield's dumb guard.
      i want to tell you my spirit is the orphan
of an extinct bird, and that when i say sorry
      it's my sorry but also the sorry of feathers,
the sorry of migrations that happen while i dream
      of falling through a burning elevator shaft.
i want to say *whoops* and blow out all the candles.
      i want to photobomb the bell curve's fat belly
and then i want to taste sadness like it is yesterday.
      i want to apologise for the moon that cried
all homecoming, whose laces came untied
      in the bramble, and who bent too long
in front of your sun. i want to tell you
      i'm trying to renounce horns, and roots and hooves.
there are so many good people queuing for sandwiches
   and heaven is somewhere between
the soup kitchen and the laughing clowns.
      when i park up, i want the wardens to witness
me in pieces. and throw the pieces to the dogs.

Sometimes I dream America

You were standing in the kitchen with your hairnet, America.
You grilled factory bacon, and watered parsley in the windowpot.
It was hot in there, America. We sweated on mattresses
next to a field of corn. We barefoot walked through bluegrasses
and barley. America, we lassoed ancient horses, yoked them
to our bedposts. We erased continents, with the butt of a rubber.
We smoked tailors in our cordoned-off rectangles, America.
We ordered Big Macs and napalm. We downloaded the world
from our couches, exploded villages from our apartment suites,
watched body counts split into a solitary pie chart.
You were standing in the kitchen with your hairnet, America.
You wrote your best love poem on a serviette, in a Tulsa
milk bar. It was folklore, America. But still we stood
in bus shelters, with supermarket bags and shotguns,
baffled and alone.

Somebody else's shoes

the sneakers i stole were waterlogged
and i wore them past tobacco plants,
past the wash house with its grungy dogs,
past the men threshing reeds by the lake.
i romped the boglands, waded through
a slick of mosquito larvae and diesel oil,
honked at the black swans, stood on
the mudbank, wrote my name in the grit.
an old taniwha smiled at me from the shadows.
just who do you think you are? he said.
and, turning down the sidewalk, my hips
began to crumble, my feet turned to cinders.

Lines

the telephone lines blow up,
along the treeless avenue.
sparks sour the night air.
like that, dogs and streetworkers
ponder the supernatural.

night is an earful of bullet holes,
a little god on either end of a chain,
making cold calls.
inside the communications centre
the desks are inconsolable.
poetry wallows between question marks.
police? fire? ambulance?
on the other end of the chain,
she reads the street sign for clues.
the hills are a signature written
in fear. deep breaths,
says the operator.

she kneels in the treeless avenue.
the telephone lines are hawks
mapping out tragedy.
stars sting the back of her throat—
police? fire? ambulance?
everywhere she looks
is a hole to something else;

their bodies, separated by flowers.

Maze

Moonless, lit only by the foxglove and the whites of his laces,
he charted the maze, looped like intestine.

A blindman tracing the face of his enemy. He chewed reeds and bulbs
and flowerstalks. He marked his chin with lilac dyes.

He drank Cabernet Sauvignon and told passers-by it was blood,
or the red magma that carried his feet, that shifted from his knuckles

when the tide went out. He stood by the rotary shed. Sometimes
he slept in the laps of milkmaids, or tossed under the belly of an
    ancient mare.

He collected fungus from the crags of claybeds,
and lined it in his shirt pockets. Insects crawled up his nostrils

and named him a little god. He knelt at the foot of a three-pronged
    road.
On every track was a pony and a chalice and incense sticks.

He watched the skyline for a sign; the villages settled like stars
in the evening light. Milky lamps blinked on and off.

Woodthrush barked carols like children. The last sun hacked
trenches in the western fields. He took the middle route,

stubbed out the incense between index finger and thumb.
Everywhere he trod, he could sense the Minotaur's grassy breath.

He hid in hay barns and made friends with the shadows
of macrocarpa trees. He could smell bull on the tongues of lilies.

He could see bull tracks in the peatbanks and the loam.
Moonless, he walked to the creek. Children barked carols

at the water's edge, like woodthrush. *Good night*, he grunted,
but the children skipped into the maze's bowels.

A blindman can tell a Minotaur by the sound of his heart,
can smell a Minotaur in eddies of darkness.

Moonless, lit by the whites of his laces, he washed his face
in the creek water. Under his two soft hands, horns.

Where we go

Everything is light, moving across
gradients. The kettle whinnies
sorry vowels while my lover
steeps into the clay. The things
I love come to me in fragments.
Her chin. Sunbeam on her wrist.

Where we dug the hole,
milkweed sprawls giddy
with monarchs, and aspens
speak of absence in hushed tongues.
There are things you cannot say
of the lost. I find myself
sobbing over each chrysalis,
cupping my mouth for grief.

The monarchs, you know,
will cross oceans in the
loneliest miracle.
Alone, in the garden,
I press a conch shell
to my ear and I can hear the
happiness of other people's lives

so far away.

Everything is light, moving away from itself.

Stranding

We were never alone, pushing up loam on a blackened beach.
We kicked our tails like we were trying to escape
the outline of ourselves. We came ashore, two by two
with our cutlasses and compasses, with our baleen smiles
and bad attitudes, with our dead-end marriages and dreams that choked
in drift nets. We were never lost. We knew the shoreline better
than we knew our own purposes. We were a quarter into lives
that stood us up from the water-break, that left us gasping
by the river mouth, blistering under wet sacking,
our eyeballs fierce with the evening sun.
We wanted the attention. We wanted to arrange ourselves
upside down and scattered like something infinite. Like stars.
We follow each other to the end of the beach
and sing something that reminds us of bone
and the million land-flowers our mothers spoke of,
and the kamikaze heritage, our fathers and their fathers,
who recognised a vague phosphorescence
and shadowed it into the salt marshes, dreaming of air.

An inventory of potions in tanka

Haloperidol
walks past the nurses' station,
hands in her pockets.

The lights gutter—small signals
to an inmate's cartoon god.

Aripiprazole
runs her fingers through her hair—
bad stereotype,

bleeds the watercooler dry.
Words stick like wrecked train cars. O.

Olanzapine shrugs,
picks through lovers like white meat,
swallows the headlines.

If there is an animal
with four stomachs, she is it.

Clozapine summons
spit and paunch, seizure and light.
She makes a small god

out of origami card.
She is the shrinking violet.

Risperidone sings
of tin men and rust hinges.
Alarm in her chest

is a hundred thousand gnats
hitting the moth lamp, head first.

   Quetiapine speaks
slow as shame. She bows to each
nurse, and falls apart

so quietly, a soft bird.
Nobody counts the feathers.

Ethics for a millennial homebody

I left a bowl of milk and fluoxetine on the patio, one time,
a cowardly sacrifice for a minor god.
These technicolour ghosts are really just the living, far away.

I can only care for the people who fit on my two hands, and most of
    those
taste and sound like me. They say Englishmen smell like clotted cream
and blood. In my dream my teeth are falling into butter.

On the television there is a man who builds wells,
and an elk, a child cobbling shoes in a factory someplace
I couldn't point to on a map. My mouth is a hole with no landmarks.
Yesterday, I held a hairdryer to my temple, like it might shatter into stars.

Some days I don't know whether I'd save the whole of Yemen
                    or my dog.
                    I know my dog
better than I know quadratic equations or meiosis or the fly spots
on the dehumidifier.
                    I know Yemen
                    like I know twenty-seven million
                    will never fit in my cupped hands.

What I mean to say is, like my dog,
I shit on everybody else's lawn and come home wagging
my dog body and thinking of Beef Strapz.

My skin smells like kibble and the marrow of small creatures.
I break into a bottle of microbeads and scrub and scrub
and sometimes I direct the showerhead away from the tenant spider

and sometimes I don't, just like that.

OK

OK sits quiet as an abscess,
just taking things in.

OK is a patient flower,
blackens when you say you won't come.

OK keeps a wall calendar of defeats
beneath a folly of Dutch windmills and yellow cakes.

OK is what you say, when you
force expectation into a paper bag
with somebody else's name on it.

*

There are three words you say
in the wet dream, but when you wake
you fold in on yourself, like a slater.

OK is what you can say
when you spot your creator in the credits that fall
like people.

OK steadies the hand inside your mouth,
to make a puppet not a fist.

OK is a placeholder for a number
bigger than a dinosaur but smaller than your sorrow.

OK knows a handful of fun facts
like heart attacks

are more likely
to happen on a Monday.

OK is a running commentary
on the extravagant mistakes that huddle
round you like nuns or volcanos.

OK is all we have.

*

There are complete sentences
in the cupboard under the stairs

Blind, they wait out
the way you open
and close your voice like a fish.

In the dream we are dumb and white
and everything that cowers between stories.

mole

It starts with a freckle.
It is in the wrong place, you see.
You'll watch commercials for Mole Maps
and make gentle notes.
Is it an irregular form,
the shape of Kazakhstan or maybe Mongolia?
Is it pedunculated? Has it an obelisk
with a copper plaque remonstrating war?
Is it globular; a series of troglodytes
with skinny dogs in the doorways?
Is it raised, like El Alto, hovering above railyards
and airfields like an hypoxic God?
Is it a black hole haloed in white?
It is in the wrong place, that's all.
You drink black tea to calm down.
You Google moles.
Your left eye is a hummingbird, quivering.
MD Online wants you to be more specific.
Is it an undulating coral coastline,
with palm trees inland?
Is it the sort of place you'd honeymoon
with lagoons and sea mammals?
Is it a dead end? Is it brown,
at the Detention Centre, with jandals
and a mouthful of rice puffs?
Is it irregular?
Or does it remind you of the photocopier's
grey aura? Is it Ground Zero?
Is it the sort of place they'd burn,
the sort of place they'd smoke you out?
It is in the wrong place, you see.
It starts with a freckle.

How I hate Pokémon but I can show restraint and just talk about my adolescence

I threw a Bulbasaur off an overbridge.
I torched a Swirlix in a Grill and Shakes diner.
I drowned a Karrablast in my laundry sink.

There are many ways to skin a Deerling.
You can use a hacksaw or a Gillette Sensor3.

You can put a Ducklett in a washing machine
on a long spin with your skid-marked panties.
You can cook a Krookodile with soy sauce
and garnish it with Solosis wedges.

*

I spent my teens
hyperventilating in elevators,
counting mites
in the carpet fibre,
yanking at emergency cords,
speculating dread.

*

Childhood axioms follow me like lost dogs.
Peter Piper picked a peck of pickled peppers.
How much wood would a woodchuck chuck?

I had to Google 'woodchuck'.
It's essentially a groundhog,

like every Wednesday
when I cross the onionweed field towards your back yard,
past the grungy dogs and washing lines,
and knock at your kitchen window.
Like every Wednesday you never answer.

*

In the bar I order a club soda for you
and a beer tower for me, even though
the restraining order keeps us metres apart.
I can feel the chemistry.

Is that a Sudowoodo in your pocket, or are you
just happy to see me?

Peanuts

I kissed you with peanut butter gums
outside the grocery store.

Anaphylaxis looks like a figure of speech—
a grown man with a foot in his mouth,
a rolling stone gathering no moss.

We matriculated, that summer,
but here you go dying, all tongues
and swiftness heading to the black woods.

I kissed you with peanut butter gums
and you were the prettiest vertebrate
I knew, gagging into sawdust.

Anaphylaxis looks like an ampersand
sitting with its claws out. Here you are,
sucking on the nozzle of the vacuum,
blue turtleneck,
forgetting mathematics
and clenching at air. You shed petals
where you kneel.

Anaphylaxis is a turn of phrase,
flaked out on the sidewalk,
gulping the exhaust fumes and waving
down cars.

Pedestrians smile with their vegetables
in shopping bags.
Golly they say and *by gosh*.
The sky reddens.
I Google how long it will take.

Counterstrike

This click click
is the heart's reloading.

Under the ceilings that hold us down
we kid around with bayonets.

Nobody is shovelling
shrapnel from the lounge.

Our mothers are making slaws in gaudy aprons.

Somewhere else bombs dissolve
the teenagers like they were

never there.
They are not
playing videogames.

Their mothers pray to gods that hide
in corners.

Ceasefire is a spring
pulled the length of a suburb.

You can hear it clamouring
a kilometre up the road.

It trades in snot and sleeplessness.
Dollar cigarettes.

Who am I to see genocide in the angles
of a pencil?

We kid around with flamethrowers
while doing arithmetic.

I wouldn't know
about anything much.

The president is tweeting about Meryl Streep

while I am peering at the world through
the scope of a sniper.

The circle of blood they make is
low resolution like in a dream I have.

Helicopters circle in pixels.

The eating of sorrow

There were days I spent gulping sky,
picking every star off the plate
with the stub of a thumb.
There were days when birds
would slide down my windpipe
and I would splutter little heartbeats,
wipe my mouth with the corner of a cloud.
There are holes in my eyes.
Photons knock against the blind spot,
received by nobody, except maybe
Achelois hiding behind an intercom,
waiting like a moon in her kitchen
for the doorbell to shatter sorrow
of hours spent lost in margarine
and newspaper. There were days
I would not stand in corners,
days where sparrows would perch
in my tear ducts and rain-pellets
would tickle my windshield of pain.
There are holes in my eyes.
At night I exit my apartment to
skinny dip in Kokytos. I swallow
galaxies of light, and stumble back
to my driveway, my stonework wall.
And I am more spent than sorry.

Husk

The girl who cops
 a feel behind the greenhouse
makes a promise—
 crosshatches her heart
with a rusted garden trowel,
 wrings out her aorta
in a bracken field,
 composts her underskirt—
the husk of somebody
 taller.
Her body is arpeggiated,
 played in pieces
that falter towards
 the empty canopy.
He knows her hesitation
 like the palm of his hand,
leaves a thumbprint
 on her cheek, the size of
a souvenir.
 There are jellybeans
at the counter of
 the abortion clinic.
There are reasons
 to pick the black jellybean.
There are reasons
 her body is not a vessel,
but a wildfire, an orange
 brushstroke amongst
grey oblongs.

fever

moving away from the orchard plots,
laundry lines that sag under macrocarpa.
moving away from the crystalline skies,
the salt-struck grasses, the train carts
and the underpasses. i astral travel
with a flannel on my head, drink litres
of holy water, chicken broth. i vomit
words into the plastic bucket, brush
the acid from my teeth. i move away,
over tussock country, along the desert
road. i chew the pillowcase. i cling
my body to the bunk. the streets
unfurl, slick with gum and cigarettes.
somebody is yelling my name. i quiver
like a sparrow. hello hello, says the
paramedic. but i am moving away from
the city lights, the steel towers.
and i shed my skin on a motorway
and i float up into the sky.

Away we go

1.
What you want is a diagram, with exit points marked
along the fuselage. You want Economy, with fifteen movie channels
and a King James Bible. You want to die after the plane,
not on the plane. You don't want to die in this poem.
You were the first of us to debunk certain doom.
You flew over Iran and the cabin tasted like egg powder and BO.
What you want is a blindfold and earplugs—layer upon layer
of Helen Keller, but discretionary. You want conditional midnight,
stars with the sort of caveats that diminish dark.

2.
If I were assembling a flat-pack of your face
I would get so far and need a Phillips-head screwdriver.
I would empty out the bureau of my life and find nothing
but loose batteries and roadmaps. I would walk to the gas station
and use their lavatory because I don't shit my nest.
I don't need a compass or a pigeon's magnetoreception
to tell me how to follow the Norfolk pines home.
I don't need a dog's bark to register the doorbell.
I don't need your face to tell me how you went away.

3.
We read the safety card on the airplane, until we realised
we could spy a landfill from a thousand feet up.
We were innocuous as dodos, dumb as brontosauruses.
Everyone could see the roll of the horizon,
the funnelled needlework of crop and tributary
at which we aimed our slight hope.
When the flight attendant moved up the aisle
with her lifejacket inflated, whistling Beach Boys,
we braced for ocean—embraced it with wide arms,
but it just slouched and did what oceans do.

4.

X-ray machines flank the passage.
I am what happiness holds to like glass.
I am just a small man losing petals. I am shucked organs.
Shards. I am the cassette melting on your dashboard.
I am other people's travelling slideshow.
I bareback ride other people's memories, just for kicks.
One day I was a hippocampus narking on its own stealth,
a seahorse remembering the fins that set him forth.
We have been so many places, and still X-ray machines
touch our bones soft as surgeon's hands,
peel the skin back like it is transitory. Like bombs lie beneath.

5.

Gull's eye view. You still don't want to die in this poem.
You don't want to put on your oxygen mask
before or after mine. You don't want complimentary candy
when the world drops altitude. But look, here we are.
Below, a mizzled seascape, acned with ships
and us somewhere up, churning cloud, and imagining
craypots, lifesavers, a cruise liner moving slow as the hour hand.
The drinks trolley grinds the aisle and I wonder
whether your version of home is a captioned dot
on a flight screen, whether you take off to stay still.

Distance

I blow kisses through the quarantine window
but the glass is double glazed.

That year, all the summer fields
are punctuated by hospitals.

I trudge the outline of a rectangle.
I trudge a worm of linoleum and bleach.

The skyline is doubled over;
elbows about its knees.

It is all you can see from the cubicle.
It is everything sad.

I keep your hairbrush for DNA.
I bring you

blackberries, frankincense,
lorazepam.

I make marionettes with my hands.
I make you the best alpaca you've ever seen.

I smuggle in fortune cookies from Wah Lee's.

You give me the thumbs-up
but every cookie is empty.

The kisses I blow make desperate Os
on the quarantine glass.

Sissy as an elephant

This is not a joke about a bogan
walking into a bar. This is not another hillbilly
taking his turn to facilitate a punchline
in Bible-belt, backwoods Boonsville.
Here is five-dollar beer and love gone to seed—
love with a split lip and broken knuckles.
This is what you find when you keep going,
when, as a wolfling, you dug that ditch
all the way from Tacoma to Texas,
when you raked the hell out of a gutter,
looked down the drain and thought you saw
a whiteboy staring back. Who are you
sitting with your Wild Turkey and Colas?
This is not a joke about the Oompa-Loompa
who peels the maraschino cherries
to pay gas to keep his Ford E-Series
crawling past the Confederate-flagged hedges,
past Joe Roughneck's sorry ghost.
This is not a joke about the rodents in the scullery,
or the buckeyes bobbing through the saloon doors.
This is not grown men huddled round pretzels
and cigarettes, talk punctuated by drags.
This is about loneliness, the way everything
is a metaphor for everything else.
The vinyl chair, the beer-haloed coasters,
the men in glass houses and the elephant
in the room, whose name badge says 'Sissy'.
The bird in the boot heels is a red herring,
but is the apple of their eyeballs,
which is a metaphor so sad it makes grown men
sob and jerk off into the same handkerchief.
There's nothing left to do but go legless
into the night, pie-eyed and hammered.

23andMe

I'm counting on proteins, washing pegs
of chromosomes, prayer beads of ATCG
in fine shark-tooth lines. It is noon
and the basin is full of Brussels sprouts.
I can roll my tongue and make a hitchhiker's
thumb, but that doesn't mean I'm happy.
I made a bracelet from saliva and
cotton swabs. I put my last dream
in a test tube and sent it to the USA.
I eat Brussels sprouts because of Ancestry.com.
I met my dead relatives in cyberspace,
sootfaced and bowlegged, and kind of like me.
They had the gene for boiled brassica.
We were all pharaohs in a past life
with golden earlobes and taxidermied cats.
But for now I'm the recessive child
rinsing a colander of vegetables,
boneless with blue eyes.

Postcard from your obese lover

I am the butter knife, not the cleaver.
You might think I'm invisible, potato
on a side plate. I'm a belly full of proverbs
about the best way to a man's heart. I can tell you
what a field of sunflowers cannot.
I'm canola oil, amber light refracting.
I can see that you're a hard yolk to split.
I'm comfort food and empty carbohydrates.
I'm mash. Macaroni. I'm a throat full
of stewed pears pushing up against
the sewer grate. I'm Fanta cans
and supermarket bags. I'm the butcher's block
and the whinnying piglet. I'm salted.
I'm the pot calling the kettle black.
I'm the fluids drained out in the basin.
You might think I'm invisible, potato
on a side plate. But I'm your reflux
and your heartburn.
I'm what passes for love.

Up here

Where seaglass meets the grassline, and the lone gull whoops,
and the shower-curtain meanders an unlit horizon,
where the estuary sucks its capillaries
into the brackish basin and back again, the storm
sets its blackened eyeball on the sleepy pier.
With a thermos of split peas and pork bone the fisherman
drops his stethoscope to the sea and listens.

The sea coughs a little, then breaks into song
about the dreadnought whose crew sip on bilge water
and chew coca leaf, who dogwatch drunk
and carve names of girls into the lonely futtocks,
while the gulls whoop and the parrot chitters.
Everyone dies, sings the sea through his rattled chest.
The dreadnought is cursed. Even the parrot.

The fisherman pulls up his stethoscope and hums
and hahs. The pier shakes its bony knuckles at the night
and the sea disrobes and stretches into the black.
The fisherman says *this might feel a little cold*
and he casts his fluorocarbon line down far enough
to reach the sea's guts. *Does it hurt*, says the fisherman
but the sea says *Up here. No, left, where my heart is.*

Stones

Do you know the way to a woman's heart is through the gallbladder?
Tenderness calcifies in the exits, squats in doorways with hairspray
and cola.

A woman's heart is bile and fat. She swallows it back, sometimes.
Sometimes she hoicks it into the sink.

A woman's heart is the kind of organ you keep in a viola case and leave
on a train. Security will blow it. Smithereens.

It's casual terrorism—a woman explodes in an art gallery. A woman
is on fire in the homeware store. A woman strips topless in Times
Square and orchestrates her own rape.

It is an exercise in logistics. A woman can't read a users' manual or
put together the flat-pack of where she is in the centre of things and
down a bit.

Do you think a woman thinks of England? No. She's conjuring the
Southwest, with canyons and cacti and jackrabbits that jostle on the
dust road. She is the road.

A woman doesn't mind that you've run her down in your pickup truck.
A woman blends in with the flora. A woman doesn't know what she
wants, what she really really wants.

Sometimes, a woman's heart is mansplained by the court judge. Why
didn't you use a clamp, the judge might say, but a woman just plays
dead.

Years from now they will say Woman like it's allegorical. They will tell Little Golden Book stories about the woman in sheep's clothing, the woman who cried wolf.

These days all the story books are empty. At bedtimes we collect gallstones in plastic cups.

All night, women pick at the glass ceiling like a scab.

Sonnet for a towerblock

Life nets and the firehoses snake the tenement,
while flames abseil down the aluminium cladding
and 11,000 miles away a small boy is mapping
the far cries, livestreamed, and hard of sentiment.

In the movie, firefighters stand about and chat.
You make milk pudding in the blaze. Twenty-four floors
swollen in the summer heat, a chest of drawers
issuing outwards. Each corridor leads to a welcome mat.

There were early mugs of tea and predawn snacks,
sunken stairwells and tweets that defied the smoke
that climbed each step, insidious as a joke

about Ramadan. The hijabs got buried in the black.
In South Kensington a cyclist saw the ash and circled back.
London is a blazed insomniac.

Since

since forgetting is not forgiving,
since we were eaten from the shins up,
by city dogs. since we were cat people,
for what it's worth,
since we knew autumn nights—
the spooked driveways,
carports with rusted bikes and old paint tins.
since we saw the terns headed north,
and knew they'd hover like ghosts
above the jetties of other people's lives.
since we knew how unhappiness
combs the twigs from your hair.
how everything good waits on its tailbone
for an adjustment of the abacus.
since forgetting is not forgiving,
since I forgot the shape of my mouth
and knew my eyes only for their sockets.
since a heart locket is not enough of a person
to hold. since we were both ovens
blowing out the fuse box. since time heals
nobody who may be bleeding out.
since what doesn't kill you,
can still fuck up your life.
even if I ached a thousand times
more than you, I'd be no more forgiving.
we wait in the ED,
for somebody to compare our wounds
to those of the patient on the table—
I tell my medical history like it is a talent,
since there is nothing better to do.

Mydriatic

the galaxy moored in the pitch of her pupil
swells and bucks. time dilates—a flower—
origami that unfolds outwards like the dream
she wouldn't tell me. sometimes I wake
with my head in my hands; sometimes I find myself
walking the farm at night, mad cows on the pyre,
embers flecking my coveralls. everything goes up
like this. or outwards. her eyeball is a bullet hole
to a heart. I eavesdrop from the outside.
I can hear beating. the machinery of a star.
the motel refrigerator. I can hear loneliness
and it reeks of bourbon and kettle chips.
everything is eggshelling at its edges.
I hold my right and left ventricles in turns.
but the eyeball is a black hole—origami
that unfolds outwards like the dream
she wouldn't tell me. everything goes up,
like this. I catch the embers on my tongue.

Tropes

There is a black horse that rides through all my poems,
zagging past the radio towers and the honked dreams that geese
   make.
On the counter my mother is fist deep in white meat and soapy water
and she might see the horse come through, or not.
There is a pantry of onions, expired and shooting green tongues,
and the horse will nuzzle them, then move on with balloons in his
   mane
and streamers in his coarse tail. Lord forgive me,
I starved that horse until he moved slow as shame
past the lindens and past the streetlamps that shout their own names.
I wrote him out of the poems. I wrote instead of white meat,
of geese that are spat in a V from South Carolina to someplace
where the horses are piebald and wet and shiny.
Sometimes, I bury my head in a foot of night and hope like hell
I'll wake cradling the limbs of somebody better.
I'm always writing the same story, with horses that haunt
the sod fields, and characters that change hairdos but hold
to their names like hope. Lord forgive me,
if I broke the horse it wasn't in my nature.
In my latest poem I slip the saddle to rinse the blood
from my gum-white hands. There are truer things than disgrace.

Rabbit

Man, I guess I had been rehearsing
my comeback all my life, but words turn to tinder
and stone. We drive through the shoulder of white bark
talking in syllables that only trees understand.
You drive with my rib in your pocket. I cannot
stomach the smell of person in these woods.
We pull up by the river, peel back the bracken,
and go down to the mooring. I swear I wouldn't
touch you with a bargepole. Man, I would run
like I do in dreams, through the chickenwire
and into the clearing. I would be met by wolves,
but I stay still, steady the ketch with a yellowed oar.
The thing with this, it's not a dream; you can tell
by the way things taste. Yesterday I chewed
a kawakawa leaf and it tasted of all the reasons
I should go. *Run, rabbit, run.*
Man, you are smaller than my thumb from here,
but you crouch on the riverbank
and name all my favourite stars like they are yours.

Export

He walks bok choy row—a green bag,
a bird gun, and a head full of ghosts.

He sells Chinese vegetables to the UK.
Water spinach, shepherd's purse, amaranth.

Everything is a derivative of cabbage,
in the same way the derivative of dog is table.

The professor cut a cabbage in half
to demonstrate the coronal viewpoint.

Look, said the professor, with his box and handsaw.
You can pass 450 volts through the human brain

and after all, it will forgive you.
You can microwave a cabbage for three minutes

and make a laxative soup. The professor
loved the Hippocratic Oath like it was his wife.

Look. But the boy was walking bok choy row
and did not know sagittal or medial,

knew instead the way the rabbit will favour
pea shoots to tong ho, knew the way night

enters the room with a polite cough,
the way the sun lumbers, spilling itself in cloverdew.

The boy knew the city enough to know
he has to creep, to tiptoe his wishes in the wells

that lead somewhere septic. The boy saw cars
lined up like Crayolas.

He saw Magenta, Cyan, Macaroni and Cheese.
He saw men on balconies of tealights and sham flowers.

The boy was a short horse in a past life,
running through the yarrow. And then in another life

he shot a swamp hen right between the eyes.
One lifetime, he was a mantis on a yam leaf,

Then he was the prayer of the mantis.

Fractures

1. She holds her fist like a bird. The knucklebones rattle. If she opens the window, she might fly—over the vegetable garden and over the gorse hedge and over streetlamps and Jim's house and the school swimming pool which smells like fear. But flight is a coward's noun. Her good hand is an anchor. It holds to arithmetic and furniture, swing sets and stars. She is greyscale. She chews the nib of the graphite pencil. It's broken. It is what it is.

2. They counted backwards from ten. *Here we come!* they said, and ran like ponies. She hid in the wash house, between the tub and the electric dryer. She was prey, and inconsequence—a small leaf blowing through a stampede.

3. What is the place between the filament and the light? It is the girl. She holds her photoreceptors like she holds her heart— loosely. She likes to think it could slip through her fingers.

4. The girl is big boned. The doctor said if she were small she might have disappeared, might have turned ghost, or a crustacean that you can see through—the gut bits and the nerves. The girl wears her bones like a badge. *Look*, she says, and animals size her up. She is too big to swallow.

5. There are breaks that chart a history of sorrow. She is broken in eleven places. Her collapsed lung and split spleen. Her ribs, her lumbar, her small hope. *What do you want to be when you grow up?* says the nurse, and the girl says *Whole; I want to be whole.*

6. How many times can it hit her? She counts the blows in twos, like it's as simple as mathematics.

7. There are animals and then there are animals. The girl is a runner. In her dreams she is a colt in the starting stalls, a wind-back toy. She knows the hundred-metre sprint like it is her body. She sleeps with her sneakers on. She is ready, always ready. The nurse with the face like sunshine says she needs to slow down, to breathe from the belly, to think of her toes.

8. The girl with the big bones does times tables in the shower. She catches herself in the mirror and spells her disgust in eleven-times-nine. She grabs at the flesh and wishes it away. Collateral meat. Ground bait for sharks. The girl can doggy paddle or breaststroke but it's not enough. She is a landlubber. The girl is not a girl to the predator below the surface, whose gum eye she cannot meet.

9. But this is not about water.

10. This is about the love that lurks in corners. The girl is sutured together, with strings that action her like a puppet. The nurse says *This will not hurt* and for the first time, it doesn't. The girl wants to go home in the nurse's handbag. She wants to fold into a wallet, or lie straight inside the cigarette tin. But the girl is big boned. She will not fit.

11. The movie ends with the girl running into the sunset. She is running to give you a happy ending. She runs past the dairy and the fruit shop and dry fields of maize. If you wait the credits out, you can see her rise, up and up. It's like the dream, but better.

Thinner.

Less.

In the next life

I'm Wile E. Coyote, who weeps at sparrows,
and can't make binoculars focus on the dull stars.
My claws are petals. Teeth are mothwings.
My homeland is ghost-bones, the silvered tongues
of afternoon evangelists. I drink chamomile tea
in front of Reverend Ike while another piano
falls onto my head or I'm hit by a passing freight train.
Sellotaped to diverging tracks, Penelope Pitstop
is scratching haiku in the railroad sand.
I'm from the wrong cartoon, she says,
and Reverend Ike rolls his eyes and offers up
a metaphysical pie-in-the-sky with clotted cream.
In the next life I'm Wile E. Coyote who weeps
at eiderdowns and tea towels. My favourite colour
is corned beef, but I eat only legumes. There is no
acid in my stomach to digest the sadness,
stalking the foot-scuffs of an intangible bird.
There are enough figments in this world
to act as handrails between facts. I chase
Roadrunner like he is speeding away,
dust clouds following him into the sunset—
a midge between cacti on a craggy horizon.
He is closer than the sky.

Boomerang

The opposite of Sorry is a man with a walking stick
who wears a cravat and eats luncheon meat on a Tuesday.

Redemption speaks in nasal tones and collects fridge magnets.
I watch her through the laundry window, and sometimes

she mouths words in a foreign language through the glass.
Outside the barbershop, Forgiveness asks for handouts

but I always carry Eftpos. Guilt waits in the carpark with
a crowbar and a whippet. Sorry, I say, Sorry.

But Sorry is too busy watching the cooking channel.
Some days I don't want to walk anywhere with mammals.

-

We play Guess Who? in balaclavas,
but they can smell the wheat in my breath.

Do you have a moustache? Somebody might say.
Are you schizophrenic?

Sometimes I think they could have saved my life
with a packet of spearmints and a quality comb.

I tell my employers I have irritable bowel syndrome
like they might like to keep it up their sleeves
for a rainy day.

Can you spell WORLD backwards, they might say.
Can you roll your tongue?

-

I have a drawer of dead batteries, like everybody else.
I am a series of good intentions.

I watched this documentary
where they put a dead greyhound
on another dead greyhound,
wet them with kerosene
and a thousand buckaroos of pedigree
went up in smoke, just like that.

When the worms eat me, I wonder whether
I'll taste of private education and Pink Batts?

Some nights I go to say
Sorry
like it might count
but Redemption is filing tax returns
on her granite countertop
and doesn't hear
the major third ascending
from the doorbell.

I shed kilos reading
Cioran in the mall

'I am displeased with everything'
                    —*E.M. Cioran*

Sometimes I go hunting
for oxytocin
in Sylvia Park,
like our love
is empty calories,
like Karen Carpenter
is our spirit animal,
like me plus you
makes something
less than a zero,
like sometimes I go
buying sentiment
that hangs
with bling-lanyards
and bangles,
or the window dresser's
mannequins
who carry small hope
in the napes
of their neck stumps.
Sometimes I go
roleplaying sweet nothings
to the cashier
in the carpark building
and mostly I am scared
of falling
for something
complicated like

mechanical barrier arms
that crush whole
torsos and spit out feet
and collarbones.
And sometimes I go
listening to customers
yabbering
about refunds and
hire purchases
and it just rubs in
the fact that
I am not
financially literate
like I can't even count
in twos or add up
blessings
on one hand.

Foreign attraction

Which country would you marry,
and which one would you shag?

I'd marry Finland. I'd blow Nicaragua. I'd shag Australia if she wore a
     paper bag.
I'd serve fried chicken to Hungary, and walk the promenade with Latvia,
howl at the moon with Mexico, tap dance on the hedgerows with Qatar.
I'd watch hentai porn with Japan, and play footsie with Bangladesh
while talking epistemology with Lebanon. I'd revisit the cartoons
of childhood with the USA, but he would spike my milk
and Yogi Bear and Felix the Cat would blacken like unwatched crops,
and the hot milk would sour in my throat. I'd say, *hey America,*
that's no way to treat a lady. And America would leave a voicemail
re-framing civil rights with a soft slurred tongue.
I'd marry the Philippines. I'd unfold the bloody clothes of Rwanda.
I'd iron North Korea's starched uniform and hiff it on the bonfire,
where Manus Island's refugees already burn. I'd flush munitions
down the public lavatories of Russia's backblocks. I'd meet
the Sudan in an alleyway, with a pistol in my pocket,
and assorted playing cards. I'd perform a sexual favour for Kosovo,
and make it Facebook official. I'd French kiss Yemen
with my windows wound up. I'd high-five Canada,
and run through the spice gardens with Jamaica,
high on crystal methamphetamines filched from New Zealand.
And America would knock four score and seven times
on my apartment door, like I was everything he'd worked
his white buttocks for, like I was the starlet of his wet dream.
And I'd play *Pussy Riot* through the intercom speaker,
while Syria would be stuffing a cigarette on the kitchen counter
and the United Kingdom would brew another cup of average tea,
then spreadeagle on the daybed, licking her English teeth
like it's the only half-decent thing to do.

Taxing the ghost

The metaphysical creditor waits on the beach
with cutlass and crook.

Let him say we lived through slim pickings,
sucking on the rinds of our better halves.

Let him say we lived with our tails between legs,
that we loved in increments.

And let him doff his sailor's hat for us
but let him wait for slippage,

the insouciant wicket-keeper,
catching spells we never cast.

He'll stand on the dunes
and read the SOS we didn't fashion
out of seawood and bladderwrack.

And there will be years when
nobody will find us.

mama scarecrow

old mama scarecrow is sackcloth on a trellis.
small figurehead on the prow of a sunk vessel,
pastoral leftovers of a conked-out kingdom,
stiff against the stink of hot lightning and corn.
scarecrow is the mama of several small birds.
she dies like children hollering across cities,
she dies like an Oldsmobile's soured engine.
she holds out her hands to the moth-strewn night.
she will give up her body heat
for a hope brittle as stars.
she will unchew the dried bulbs of history,
spit them at the foot of her post.
old mama says history is just a woman
waiting for a man to come home.
or it's the unblinking testimony
of field crows, picking through the eyeballs
of other things. old mama says some days
history is a small child throwing its toys
down a ravine, only to wish them back a tantrum later.
there are days I spy old mama through the roll-up door.
I say, look old mama, I will ride shotgun
by fields of ammonium sulphate.
we'll smoke Lucky Strikes and pick lost tennis balls
from the aisles of corn.
and old mama will hang there, all hessian and cloth.
and she will receive my pulse like a gunshot,
and she will worship the cropped pastures
she cannot run.

Owling

Beasts—we tuck our talons into shirt pockets,
wring the marrow from our gamey pillowcases.
A bloodbath in a plastic vanity,
connective tissue a makeshift pabulum,
Power ballads sharpened to switchblades in our skinny throats.
Our tapering voice. Our vowels turned to clot.
The fish flapping on the knifeboard, or hanged
in the smokehouse. Look, here is a bouquet of nerves,
a prayer where you have a cameo role. I am saving
containers. One day I will fill them with the better part of
    intimacy—
your hazel eyes that unpick me, bone by bone.
Your feeble hands—burger, chowder, blackened roe.
We are nothing but motion, small saccades
of two solitary skulls. We map the territory, like it is ours alone.
We stamp dimples in the sooted sky. Love—
we are two owls in the magnolia tree;
we are the white meat waiting and softening like fruit,
only to rattle the small hearts of city mice. Beasts—
we catch the moonlight in absent nests.

Notes

In lieu of flowers, bring weeds. Bring bushels of nettle,
bring the knotted saltgrass, bring gorse and bog mosses.

Come, pray in the warbling amphitheatre.
The forest knows a little god who thinks slowly

and picks the grasshoppers from his shower curtain,
who grows a little uglier every day, but kinder.

In lieu of angels, bring microbial forebears.
Bring a platter of the sludges we rose from.

Bring things with hoof and things with tail.
Bring carnivores, who cannot help themselves,

thumbing through internal organs like a dictionary.
Bring a fistful of the promises you couldn't keep,

an audience of the people you could not love,
and the people who could never love you.

Bring a chain of aspens. Bring roadside fires.
Bring a torch and a head full of batteries.

In lieu of confetti, we ask that you bring photons,
bring the shadows that scuff the asphalt.

Bring the thing you cannot touch.